ebb & flow

déjà rae

ebb & flow

Cover Art by Carly Grider

As I sit here and write to you, I am anchored back into my own convictions. I am reminded of the many truths I've come to know over the years.

Growth
   does not follow
      a linear pattern.

We progress and we recess.
We learn, we forget, we hurt,
and we learn all over again.

We ebb and we flow.

A constant uphill battle
with valleys throughout the journey.

So, thank you,
because as I sit here and write to you,

I also write to myself.

Sometimes it rhymes- sometimes it won't
Sometimes I smile- sometimes I don't
Sometimes there's sunshine- sometimes there's rain
Sometimes it's happiness- sometimes it's pain
Some days you love me- some days you can't
Some days you take- some days you plant

Some days I ebb- some days I flow

But with every season,

I always grow

Seasons

Season 1

Lonely

I've always felt deeply misunderstood by most.

Sure, I've relished in the luxuries of human safe havens
from time to time, but only to realize,
emotional refuge is in fact,
fleeting.

The remarkable pain of feeling unseen has, and always
will, reverberate through my innermost being. The type
of loneliness that is not reliant upon the number of other
people in the room.

But instead, the direct result of the daunting realization
that there is not, and may never be, another human that
fully understands me.

Am I a writer because I'm lonely?

Or am I lonely because I'm a writer?

Years have passed yet my feelings for you have remained.

I wonder whether it's my own mind, yearning to rewrite the conclusion of our love story.

Or I wonder if it's fate, if it's the unspoken words that echo into each other's souls, where love knows no distance and time belongs to the cosmos.

I wonder if the moon, the sun, and the stars are all conspiring, transmitting every sweet word to me that you've swallowed.

Maybe the vibrations of this vast world will know no end other than the end of us.

Me and you, finally together as one.

One, two, three

> *How many drinks will it take for you to love me?*

Four, five, six

> *How many more to get your fix?*

Seven, eight, nine

> *It's time to leave, you say you're fine.*

Ten and then eleven

> *God, please don't take my daddy to heaven.*

Maybe one day
It will all make sense
Why you came
And why you left

Why the love
That brought me life
Came from the same hand
That twists the knife

Maybe one day
I'll understand
That homes collapse
When built on sand

That love withers
And turns to dust
That people depart
And memories rust

Questions I'll never ask

Do you miss my honey skin?
Or what about my lips?
Do you miss the way I'd hold you close,
Your hands, down my hips?

Do you regret the time we shared?
Did you forget the way it felt?
Do you think about me often?
Do you hope I'm doing well?

Do you crave for my affection?
Do you care about my life?
Do you talk to someone else?
Do you look into their eyes?

Do you hope for my return?
Are you sad to see me go?
Do you miss my honey skin?

I guess
I'll never know.

I think we often look for pieces of ourselves within other people.

We feel a hint of loneliness, a taste of something missing, and we assume the answer is in the hands of another human.

But maybe loneliness is exactly where we're supposed to be. Maybe the missing ingredient has always been inside us, aching to be discovered.

Maybe loneliness is the exact foundation we need to finally begin to put all the pieces together.

As much as we want to share our sorrow and give our grief away, the enduring truth prevails,

We were not meant to heal that way.

Healing comes from the lonely tears, the silent pain, and the empty bed. It slithers its way into our lives and nudges our skin to shed.

It comes as a thief in the night, ready to steal our joy, leaving footprints of pain. It deepens our cracks and twists our bones, forcing the poison to drain.

Healing wounds us and revives us, it pierces and it repairs. It pours love into the void and brings hope into our prayers.

So if you feel as though you're aching, paralyzed with all that weighs,

Please remember my dear friend,

Growth happens on the hard days.

Allow people to walk out of your life.

Save your energy for those that want to stay.

Trust me,

It will all make sense one day.

Do not let the cold world turn you to ice.

It takes a certain kind of strength to continue to offer
love in the face of mistreatment.

It takes a certain kind of capacity to continue to give
grace in the face of selfishness.

It's not always easy to have a soft heart.

But I can promise you this,

love always wins.

And if you are always full of love,
you will always be winning.

I've learned that there is no one that can really fill the void inside of you except for yourself.

I've learned that people are breathtakingly beautiful and dreadfully disappointing all at the same time. I've learned that your dreams and aspirations often require deep healing and raw honesty.

I've learned to be more patient; with people and with myself. I've learned to slow down a bit; to just take it all day by day when life starts to feel overwhelming.

I've learned that you must make a home in yourself. You must depend on your own intuition. You must follow every crazy path that comes your way with hopes that maybe it will work out this time.

Most importantly, I've learned to just keep going, to keep trying, to keep loving, to keep giving, to keep hoping.

I've learned that this life may not always follow your plan, but nonetheless, everything is divinely placed.

Season 2

Broken

I worry a lot for someone
    that has so much faith.

I question a lot for someone
    that has so much conviction.

I fear a lot for someone
    that has so much hope.

I have one foot in my brokenness
    and one foot in my breakthrough.

What happens when your pleasure becomes your pain?

When the one you love is also the one that brings the rain?

When their absence sends lightning piercing through your veins, but with one kiss a shot of dopamine bleeding in the brain.

I can't restrain

I can't abstain

I'll take the pain

Light me in flames

Because I don't want to be sane

if that means I can't rest in your rain

Is it safe for me to be happy?

Little One

Just a tiny cell you are
floating around

Yet the weight you carry
too heavy to bear

Just a child myself
weak and frail

How can I carry you?

One imprudent act
producing life or death

What will it mean for you?

You scream,

"Mama, don't leave me
give me a chance"

Broken and lonely,
I scream back,

Forgive me, little one

I agonize in pain
thinking maybe there's a way

I can die

but you can live

But the Doc says it's time
so, I say goodbye

and hope to die

I'm sorry, little one

To my baby sister

What's it like there in the clouds?
Is all they say true?
Do the trees taste like love?
Do the mountains sound like blue?

Do the rivers reflect the past?
Does all the pain disappear?
Will the fog ever cease?

Is it better than down here?

Are you watching over my journey?
Are you disappointed in my life?
Have you met my little one?
Is she safe?
Is she alright?

Can you tell Him that I'm sorry?
Can you tell Him I was alone?
Can you ask if He still loves me?

Is it too late to come back home?

If I had known that was the last time I would see you,

Maybe I would have hugged you a little tighter

Maybe I would've spoken a little nicer

Maybe I would've loved you with all my fire

Resilience is bred in my blood

The blood of the family vein
From years of buried trauma
Generations of silent pain

Is that why it feels so heavy?
Does all this weight belong to me?
Has gravity corrected it's course?
Transmitting the pressure over me?

I'm trying to overcome
Attempting to break the curse
But I feel shackled to the past
Burdened by my birth

But just as trauma has been passed down
Resilience runs through my veins
I am looking for the light

I *will* break every chain

But,
how can I learn
to not associate love with pain?

When the only love I know,
is the kind that brings the rain.

His Light

And when I thought I wouldn't make it
I saw His light
Beaming from the sky
Sparkling bright

He took my hand
He guided me through
He opened my eyes
He expanded my view

His spirit- soft as the clouds
Where heaven resides
His voice- strong like the wind
Tumbling by

His presence- divine and sacred
Unlike anything yet
His cross- holy and eternal
Relieving my debts

He told me- I am love
I was made in His image
And the life I see now
He has not yet finished

He told me to have hope
In His heavenly plans
And that the worth of my life
Is not up to man

So, I put down my worries
I wiped my tears
Because His presence was stronger
Than all my fears

I sat in His love
As I soaked in His grace
And now wherever I go
I look for His face

Because a moment with the Lord
Will change your life
He will give you His power
He will take on your fight

He will clear out the fog
He will restore your sight
All you must do

Is look towards His light

It is safe for me to be happy.

Put it down and let it go.

When you wake up in the morning, paralyzed with the memory of them,

put it down and let it go.

When the thought of them feels like boulders on your shoulders, knots in your guts, and pain through your veins,

put it down and let it go.

If, with every step you walk, you feel the weight of their absence placing pressure on your pace,

put it down and let it go.

You do not need to stay shackled to your suffering.

Put it down and let it go.

I look around in awe
At the beauty that surrounds me
I feel my spirit smile
I thank God that I'm happy

My heart's been bruised and beaten
My bones, brittle and broken
What a life it is
To drown in all the emotions

But my pain is not in vain
And though my troubles may never cease

I still close my eyes and thank God

For granting me *His* peace

Do not settle in your suffering.
Do not make a home in your heartache.

Now hear me out, I am not asking you to steer clear of
sadness. I am not discrediting the gravity of a heavy
heart.

Grief is a very real, human emotion; one that penetrates
our soul and leaves us paralyzed with pain.

You cannot avoid your agony.
You cannot escape your heartache.

In fact, you *must* confront it. Allow the pain to pierce
through your skin and run through your veins. Allow
your tears to flow, as they water your soul and grow
roots in your resilience.

Feel your sadness, deeply and woefully.

But once you have indulged, once you have wallowed in
the weight, you *must* kiss it goodbye and let it go.

Sadness was never supposed to be your shelter.

It was meant to be a transitory season, one where lessons
are learned and growth is gained.

So please, kiss it goodbye now and let it go.

Season 3

Realizations

Growth feels like a wrench in my heartstrings

Plucking out the ugly
and staring it straight in the face

Soaking in the pain
while pushing on the bruises

Tearing at my flesh
while twisting my bones

The demons I've tucked away for years
now come eye-to-eye

My ego bubbles up to the surface
scorching hot
after years of fueling its fire

Growth feels like soaking my wounds in the rain
It feels like lightning through my veins
Like burning in the flames
Like the weight of every chain

I guess that's why they call them growing pains

You don't really want *me*

You want the warmth of my thighs and the touch of my
skin
You want my presence to make you feel peace within
You want the late-night love and the deep conversations
You want my focus, my mind, and all my dedication
You want my fingers through your hair and my heart in
your hands
You want my soul to submit to all your demands

You want to feel a love that will set you free
But the problem is

You don't really want *me*

I don't really want *you*

I want the emotional crutch and the mental stimulation
I want your body to make me feel every sensation
I want you to touch me softly and to kiss me lightly
I want you to protect me from my pain and hold me
tightly
I want your presence, your support, and all your
affection
I want our souls to intertwine, a divine connection

I want to feel loved through and through
But the problem is

I don't really want *you*

But when do I give up the fight?

When do I throw in the towel and call it a night?

When do I decide to leave?

When do I pack up my bags and prepare for my grief?

I gave you pieces of me
Each one a part of my past
I thought maybe this would be it
Maybe you'd be the one that lasts

I crashed my soul into your chest
I laid my heart inside your hands
I melted my body into yours

But I built a love out of sand

I closed my eyes and jumped,
Putting faith into my fall
I thought that you would catch me
I thought that I'd stand tall

But when our love hit the ground
My pieces shattered everywhere
My soul crushed into fragments
My heart strangled without air

So here I am again in pieces
With only myself to console
Maybe next time before I jump

I'll be sure that I am whole

We can't change people.

But we can love them in a way
that helps them grow.

And sometimes that means
letting
go.

A lesson learned

I want to hug you with my words
I want to take away the pain
I want to fill you with my soul
I want to cover up the rain

I want to help you spread your wings
I want to do all the nice things
I want to water you like spring
I want to treat you like a king

I want to teach you how to grow
I want to kiss you with my love
I want to hold you in my arms
I want to shield you from above

But no matter how hard I try
To mend *your* cracks with *my* glue
The truth lingers in my heart,

That *I* can't fix you.

He says things will change, but the truth stays the same.

As long as you continue to justify his actions, as long as
you continue to tolerate his disrespect, and as long as
you continue to welcome him back into your bed, he will
never change.

People cannot facilitate growth in the same environment
that they've exhibited toxicity.

You may see change for a few days, maybe even a few
weeks.

But loved one,
the timer is ticking
the bomb is bubbling
and each subsequent explosion
will become greater
and more destructive.

Please walk away before he blows you into pieces.

It's time you choose yourself.

He doesn't *really* want you.

Sweet girl, if you find yourself hollowed out, entirely emptied after digging for his love, please know, he doesn't *really* want you. If you're scraping the barrel for bits, pleading for the tiniest of affections, sweet girl, please note, he doesn't *really* want you. If he has habitual seasons of absence that leave you feeling anxious and confused, sweet girl, please notice, he doesn't *really* want you.

Us girls, we seek to justify their actions, we make excuses for their absences, we defend their deficiencies. But sweet girl, when you settle for anything less than you innately deserve, you cheat yourself of your potential. You allow yourself to become shackled to stagnation.

You become chained to a love that caters to convenience.

Sweet girl, free yourself.

Free yourself for a man who will *really* want you.

You deserve someone that is sure about you.

You deserve someone that knows what they want.

You deserve someone that has the capacity to love you to the lengths that you love others.

There is already a lot of uncertainty in this life.

You deserve someone that is sure about you.

If he doesn't want you,

Do not drown in the rejection.
Do not allow him to write the coding of your worth.
Do not measure your merit through the lens of his
perception.

You are whole, you are worthy, and you are loved just as
you are.

Any man that does not see your light was not meant to
be in your life.

You do not have time for anyone
that does not have time for you.

Let me say that again.

You do not have time for anyone
that does not have time for you.

There's a lot more to this life than falling in love with someone else.

Dear friend, the purpose of your life is to fall in love with yourself.

There are pieces of you aching to be discovered.
There are parts of you waiting to be uncovered.

There are experiences to be had, people to meet, places to go, lessons to learn. Open your eyes, expand your view, spread your wings, and live your life.

Learn what you love and learn what you don't. Take art classes and music lessons and discover all the things that make your heart beat deeper.

And please remember, the journey of your life does not require a companion.

All you must do is decide that you are enough.

That your existence is enough.

That this life is enough.

I'm learning to let go of pain with tender forgiveness and gratitude.

I'm learning that every bitter goodbye is an opportunity to learn more about myself. I'm learning that I don't have all the answers, but nonetheless, I've committed myself to find truth in all things. I'm learning that my love has the capacity to heal. And even when that love has been used and abused by others, I'm beginning to see that the seeds I plant will always become fruitful with time.

I'm learning how to move on without an apology and how to forgive when my wounds are still open. I'm learning that growth is painful, but the discomfort is always worth it. I'm learning to see the best in people, but never at the expense of my own wellbeing.

I'm beginning to accept that this life will inevitably have a rhythmical flow of good moments and bad moments. That some days, I'll feel enamored by all people and all things, while others will leave me aching for intimacy.

I'm beginning to see, with clear lucidity, that love always wins in the end.

Love for yourself, love for others, love for this world.

Season 4

Decisions

I sat there on the bed with you at 3am, listening to you say that you couldn't be with me, but the words dripping from your lips didn't quite mirror the light in your eyes.

I knew you better than that.
I knew that you wanted me.

I knew that if you would have just given yourself permission to feel, you would have fallen deeply in love with me.

And you knew that too.

Does it scare you that I see you?
Is that why you ran away?
Does the truth make you tremble?
Does my fire make you afraid?

Well that's okay,
Run away
I'll see you one day
And I know you'll say,

You weren't the man I deserved
You couldn't handle my heart
You were so caught up with being scared
You decided to hide in the dark

But in the dark, you were more afraid,
Shivering with no sight
And in that moment, you realized

What you needed was my light.

Not everyone will have the capacity to appreciate you.

The most beautiful works of art in this world, the sweetest and rarest of delicacies, will never be appreciated by someone who lacks the depth to discern their value.

If someone has yet to reach your level of lucidity, they will not welcome your wisdom. They will not be inspired by your insight. They will not value your vision.

Do not dim your light chasing what is still in the dark.

Beautiful boy

Please take the time to look at yourself
to reflect on what you really need
I know the world has hardened you
and made you adamant to believe

That a man like you, strong and proud,
may never show his fears
That emotion is a sign of weakness
and you must always swallow your tears

But beautiful boy, what makes you strong
is the disposition of your soul
The fact that God made you powerful
and capable in *every* role

You are stable and steady, firm and fierce
and courageous to no end
You are kind and sweet, gentle and soft
and suited to transcend

The scripts of society,
the way the world tells you not to embrace
The feelings of your soul
and the power of your grace

So please, beautiful boy, lay your head on my lap
let me take you under my wing
Let me show you that your emotions

are precisely what make you a king

A Letter to You

I'm happy to hear you're doing so well.

I'm happy to hear all your dreams are coming true.
I'm happy to hear you've been so successful in all your
endeavors, but I can't help but wonder if you are happy
too.

I wonder how you *really* are. I wonder how your heart is
and where your mind is at. I wonder if you take time to
sit down in the mornings and reflect on life while you
drink your black coffee. I wonder what books you're
reading and what movies you're watching and I wonder
what new project has your heart beating deeper.

I wonder if you've found someone else to share your
mind with. I wonder who she is, and if she's nice, and I
wonder if she wonders about you the way that I *always*
do.

I wonder if you miss me.

And I wonder if you wonder about me too.

Please heal your wounds.

Talk to those who have hurt you.

Talk to those who you have hurt.

Shed
your
skin,

And move forward.

It takes a whole man to love a whole woman.
It takes a whole woman to love a whole man.

It takes a whole human to love a whole human.

Do not break
your
self
into
p i e c e s
trying to love someone
that has not yet come to completion.

If you want half love

You'll have to find another heart
I don't give my love in pieces
I don't give my love in parts

If you want some empty kisses
You'll need to look somewhere else
I don't need your sweet nothings
I can fully love myself

If you're looking for a fix
If you need a loving touch
You can find another woman
I am not your lustful crutch

If you're longing for a fill
If you need some satisfaction
You should look within yourself
Instead of searching for distractions

I am not your toyed attraction
I'm not a sexual transaction
I don't heed to your reactions

I don't give my love in fractions.

Be sweet
but set boundaries.

This is the only way to
love others
while also
loving yourself.

Leading with my heart has allowed me to experience the
fullness of life.

The deepest friendships.
The most transformational experiences.

Yet, it has also caused me to feel the heaviest grief.

The hardest goodbyes.
The most painful heartbreaks.

But through it all,
I can still say with certainty,

It is much better to live a life feeling everything
than nothing at all.

What if we stopped running away from pain?

What if we accepted that hurt is merely another human emotion, one that will inevitably ebb and flow all throughout life? What if we decided to unshackle ourselves, open the doors to our caged hearts and allow life to gently flow through us?

What kind of people would we meet?
What type of experiences could we have?

Years from now, when our bodies are frail and our days are numbered, will we look back on our lives and take pride in our closed hearts? Will we be grateful for the forfeited relationships? The missed opportunities? The swallowed confessions of love?

Will we regret having loved
or will we regret having lost?

I think every defining moment in our life- every blessing, every hardship, every heartbreak- has been perfectly placed.

Perfectly planned out to create the map that ultimately guides us towards who we are really meant to be. And though our journey has a definite endpoint, I think there are a countless numbers of paths that can lead us to that very end.

Some routes may be more challenging, yet also more fulfilling, while others may be easier, but lead us to live a life half-full.

Nevertheless, each will guide us to the ultimate end, to the expiration of our ethereal bodies, to the demise of our life story.

So in these moments of clarity we ask:

Which path is worth it?

If death is certain, which it surely is, which path should we take? Is it the one which leads us through darkness, living in blissful ignorance, unscathed by truth itself?

Or is it the path that is crystal clear, forever evolving, yet requiring an open heart and raw vulnerability?

I think that's ultimately the decision that we all face.

Will I allow pain in my heart to experience the fullness
of life?

Or will I live with a caged heart, perpetually protecting
myself from the rawness of reality?

Every route will inevitably lead to the end, so it's for us
to decide how we'd like to live before our time runs out.

Season 5

Empathy

I think I've seen growth

Then you slither your way back into my sight

And in that moment of magnetic silence

I look at you, and I see

My light
My fight

All my wrongs
And all my rights

My deepest desire
My guilty delight

I still want you in my life

Sometimes I wish that you would fall in love

Just so I could let you go
I wish you would tell me that you love her
Just so I could know

That the what-ifs, could-be's, and imaginings
of you and me
Are only in my dreams
And in reality, I'll see
That it's time to set you free

But you and me, in my mind,
Is all that I have left
I don't want to erase you
I'm not ready to forget

Yet the longer that you linger on my lips
And loiter in my thoughts
The more I lose myself to you
The more I grieve all that I've lost

Because losing you and losing me
Feels like drowning in a loveless sea
And in this lifetime, I can't foresee
A way that I can love you- and love me

So I wish that you would fall in love
So I can finally be done
Tell me that you love her

Tell me I'm not the one

I never learned how to tiptoe around love.

I never understood how to separate passion and
connection. I don't know how to settle on the surface,
and I don't want to know either. I love raw vulnerability
and uncensored conversation. I don't want to *talk* to you;
I want to *know* you. I want to drown in your thoughts
and submerge into your mind.

I desire a connection that transcends the superficial.

My bones ache for intimacy.
My heart craves for humanity.
My soul yearns with an affinity
for all people and all things.

I never learned how to tiptoe around love.

There's a common sentiment- that the person who cares the least has the most power.

But what is power then?

Is power pretending that we don't care when we really do? Is power choosing to walk away rather than choosing to open up? Is power indifference? Indecision? Ambivalence? It is the dreams we give up because we're too scared to fail? Is it the people we lose touch with because we're too prideful to reach out?

What is it then?

What kind of power do we achieve when we numb ourselves to love?

What kind of life do we create when we reject the very things our hearts desire?

I will continue to believe in people even if that means
I will be eternally disappointed by them.

Because that's what life is.

Love and grace for others.
Love and grace for ourselves.

The perpetual cycle of loving

and letting go.

You are always winning.

Every time you open your heart- you win.
Every time you surrender to love- you win.
When you see the best in people- you win.
When you care the most about others- you win.

Do not let the disappointment make you feel otherwise.

You have won.

What Love is To Me

Love is coffee in the morning
and breakfast at 3
Love is a bed full of secrets
and a shelter for free

Love is a tired smile
with an innocent touch
It's a kiss on the collarbone
with a full body blush

Love is timeless and selfless
and rooted in truth
It's the rediscovery of the innocence
we lost in our youth

Love is a present of presence
It's a piece of peace
It's a gift from God
One of life's greatest treats

Love is playful, patient
priceless and pure

It's the beginning
and the end
It's the pain

and it's the cure

There is nothing more beautiful than passion.

It is a heavenly trait to feel deeply and boldly towards life, to care earnestly about the ways of the world, to love all people and all things with every fiber of your being.

People are naturally drawn towards your light.
They are in love with your energy.

Your love captivates, and it intoxicates.

Your pour is large, and your passion runs deep, which requires a level of profound sensitivity and vulnerability.

As you flow through life, many people will feel awake around you. You will drive them to new depths and call them to new capacities. You will unlock new levels in their life; you will guide them towards true healing and growth.

However, there will come a point when you realize that there are many people incapable of reciprocating your shine. There are many that cannot love with your intensity.

Do not feel disheartened. Do not feel as though you are hard to please. You require more, you expect expansion, you crave true connection. The level of intimacy that you desire is one that many are unable to reach.

You are the rarest of gems, a wonder of the world.

Do not settle in the slightest, and do not comply with complacency.

The right people will always find you.

You may plant a seed
Everywhere that you go
But it is not your role to water it
And watch it grow

Share your truths
Spread your light
But set your limits
And know your rights

Plant your seeds
Then kiss them goodbye
Give it to God

Allow *Him* to supply

Don't be *too* concerned with the actions of others.

Truth is, regardless of what you may do and despite how hard you may try, you cannot and will not have ultimate control over the behaviors and beliefs of another person.

Though your intentions may be pure, it is unnatural to force someone to act according to what *you* believe is right.

Every person must learn for themselves.
Every person must grow at their own pace.

So please, do not drain yourself worrying about the ways of the world. Instead, use that energy to focus on yourself. Amplify your own intentions, attitudes, and behaviors. Spend time being the person you would like to see in others.

Your pure and authentic energy will have a greater impact than any degree of control ever will.

To all my empaths

What a beautiful gift God has deposited within you.

To be an empath is to deeply experience and absorb the emotions of the world around you. This profound sense of empathy is intended to be much more than a fickle feeling- it is meant to be a catalyst for change.

You are the embodiment of light and insight.
You are a shoulder to lean on, a hand to hold, a heart to comfort.

And though your gift comes wrapped in grace, as with everything in life, we must learn how to harmonize our abilities with our boundaries.

You must determine when to soak in the sorrows and when to tune out and take care of yourself. Just because the current of your heart runs deep and wide, does not mean you must stop to water every seed.

It is essential that you treat yourself with the same supply of consideration that you have for others.

Please, sweet soul, set limits for yourself, and learn when to dwell in your own delight.

If someone is unable to meet at your level,
do not step down to meet at theirs.

Whether that be emotionally, intellectually, or
spiritually- do not compromise your own standards to
please what you have already overcome.

In this life there are invisible levels of consciousness-
ones that concern the mind, body, and soul. To unlock
new layers, we must continually and sacrificially lay
down our ego and reflect on our lives with tender
honesty and compassion. This continual process allows
us to operate at a higher frequency, one in which our
soul breaks through the confines of our ego and
smoothly levels up.

Those who have not yet conquered their current state of
consciousness, those whose souls stay stuck in
stagnation, are fundamentally incapable of meeting us
where we are.

We cannot pull them up to our level;
they will only end up dragging us down.

So please, *strive to meet your match- not your project.*

Save your energy and dignity for those that can meet you
where you are.

Season 6

Letting Go

I saw you in my dreams last night

I didn't know what to say
I guess my pain demanded attention
I couldn't look the other way

I wish I could say it was a nightmare
But I was glad to see your face
You told me everything I always wanted
As if all the hurt had just erased

We smiled and we touched
It was the most awake I've ever felt
I thought maybe we could stay there
In the dream, we would melt

But as the morning sun came up
I had to let you go
I suppose a piece of you in my dreams

Is all I'll ever know

I guess
It's time to let you go now.

My heart has held onto every thread of you since the day you left my life. I suppose saying goodbye was never my choice, so instead, I chose to hold on, to relish in the idea that maybe one day our timing would align, that maybe one day our paths would intertwine.

But I guess
It's time now to let you go.

The scraps of you I've grasped onto are dissolving more with each passing day. I can no longer see your face or visualize your smile. I forget the way you smell and the way your hands feel flowing down my spine.

So I guess
It's time to let go.

Not because I want to, but because there's no longer a part of me that can remember any piece of you.

You can love someone from afar.

You can appreciate their existence from a distance.

There are people in this world that come into our lives for only a season of time. They shake up what we know about love and challenge us to grow outside of ourselves.

But oftentimes, we don't end up with these people. We say goodbye, and we go our separate ways, and that is okay.

People are not promised.
Not everyone is meant to stay.

Throughout life, we will create connections that will be fleeting, yet also foundational in crafting us into who we're really meant to be. And just because we can't share our lives with these special souls, does not mean that we must stop sending them love.

Wish them peace,
Wish them good fortune,
Pray for them.

Even though they were not destined to stay in our lives, their sweet memory may reside in our hearts.

A prayer for you

I close my eyes and pray to God
that his angels keep you safe

I pray to God he holds you tight
with every warm embrace

I pray he makes your dreams come true
while directing all your paths

I pray he makes the mountains move
and allows the storms to pass

I pray he grows you into the man
I always knew you could be

I pray he shows you what real love is
giving you endless joy for free

I pray to God he loves you
in all the ways I never will

I pray he eases the pain
of losing a woman
you couldn't fulfill

The more I've let go of the need to be loved by you, the more I've fallen in love with myself.

For many years, I held onto half-love because it was the only love I thought I could find.

I believed half-promises and swallowed half-lies. I gave half-truths and accepted half-efforts.

I lived my life in half.

And not because I wanted to, but because I figured half-full was better than absolutely empty.

But what I found is that the emptiness wasn't so vacant after all. Waiting there in the well was myself, aching to be discovered.

Pleading with me, asking if *I* could ever be enough.

If he wants you- you'll know

Because he will love you in a way that makes you grow

Your roots will stretch, your flowers will flow

Through rain and through shine- his devotion will show

Do not chase chemistry over character.

Because chemistry won't wake up at 3am to console you in your heaviest grief.

Attraction may not choose to love you on the good days and the bad days.

Sparks stop flying when life becomes riddled with reality.

Do not assign your intentions to other people.

Not everyone has your heart.

You don't need to convince someone to love you.

The person for you will get weak in the knees from the thought of your smile. They will cross bridges and move mountains- they will go the extra mile. The person for you will wake up Sunday mornings and brew coffee as they thank God for your life. They will pack backpacks, make lunches, sweep floors, and fold laundry- they will kiss you goodnight. The person for you will love you always, every day and every week. They will show it to you and they will never retreat.

So please listen when I say,
The undeniable truth,

You don't need to convince someone to love you

Because the person for you
Will already do it

In every pursuit.

Please don't break your heart trying to force a
relationship to work.

Oftentimes, we exhaust ourselves, we waste our time,
we drain our own energy trying to fight for someone that
is simply not meant for us.

If your relationship feels draining, depleting, or
debilitating, please consider what it is that you *really*
want.

Do you want a love that revives
or a love that restrains?

Do you want a love that supports
or a love that suppresses?

The thing is, we don't always pick the right person to
love. Falling in love comes in the innocent moments of
euphoria, when we forsake our minds and follow our
hearts instead. And though our love-drunk intoxication
may shoot us to the stars at a moments notice, we will all
eventually come crashing down, burdened with the
hangover of reality.

So ask yourself:

Does your relationship stimulate growth
or does it shackle you in stress?

Does it inspire you to be a better person
or does it require you to dim your light?

One day you will meet someone who gets it.

Someone who gets you. Someone who loves you with every vibration in their body. Someone who sees your worth and understands your needs.

The love that you will have for one another will be fluent and flowing. It will change you, and it will challenge you. It will drive you to new depths and call you to new capacities.

Hold on to this love, for it will not wither with the weather nor will it dry up through a drought.

You don't need closure.

You don't need to wait around for someone to tell you why you weren't enough for them. You don't need to sit back and listen to all the things that went wrong. You don't need to wake up every morning with a naive hope that their name will finally appear on your phone.

Stop giving them the control.

Decide today that you are enough. Decide today that although it didn't work out, new and beautiful things are on their way. Decide today that the only person that will have a hold on your heart and control over your life- is yourself.

Please, loved one, do not wait around for them to disappoint you yet again.

Give yourself closure and move forward.

The truth is beautiful things often come to completion.

It wasn't that the relationship ended or that the job was terminated or that your loved one departed from your world.

What if instead, every time our life reached a turning point, every time we were called to let go, we understood that this season in our life, that this person in our life, has simply come to completion?

We have learned what we were destined to learn. We have created the necessary experiences to launch us to our next level. We have felt devotion and pain and passion, and through this, we have discovered bigger and more beautiful versions of ourselves.

But now- it is simply time to let go. It is time to accept that not all beautiful things will last forever. The mission was completed, the purpose was fulfilled, the lesson was learned, the journey was made perfect.

The truth is, when we begin to see the people and moments in our life as transitory, we free ourselves to fully soak into every piece of our world. We appreciate every exchange, every conversation, every smile, laugh, and fleeting moment, because we know, in the depth of our hearts, that all beautiful things will one day come to completion.

Season 7

Self-Love

For a long time, I thought you were everything that I craved.

There were so many nights I looked for you in other people, questioning how I could ever be without you.

Day by day, you built a home in my mind.
Missing you became part of my genetic code.

Until one day, I stumbled upon a love that offered me more than you could ever give. A love that transcended everything that I had ever known. A love so pure and so gentle, the only kind that could never be taken away.

It turns out I was never really missing you.

I was missing myself.

If we don't practice self-love, we will search for that love elsewhere.

We will assume that the love we crave is in the hands of another human. We will betray ourselves, put others on a pedestal, and lower our self-worth just to grasp at scraps of affection.

Sweet friend, the love you are looking for is inside of you.

Keep digging.

What does loving yourself look like?

Setting boundaries.
Do not allow people in your life to treat you with disrespect. Communicate openly about what you will and will not tolerate.

Speaking positively over your life.
Compliment yourself daily.
See the intrinsic beauty that you were born with.
Remind yourself of your unique skills and capabilities.

Exercising your mind, body, and spirit.
Work towards the goals you have set for yourself.
Take steps every day to become your ideal self.

Creating from your heart.
Invest in the things that give you peace.
Spend time with yourself, doing what you love, while honoring your truest self.

Beautiful girl,

You are far more exquisite
than the way your chest meets your breasts
Your soul tells a story more fascinating
than your status ever will

Your heart, stronger and smoother
than his hands down your thighs
And the way you speak, blesses more people
than your lips could ever touch

Because beautiful girl,

You are so much more
than the shape of your breasts
and the curve of your hips

You are the strength of the sun
and the power of the winds

You move mountains with words
and create valleys with hymns

Beautiful girl,
with the beautiful skin,
the beauty in you

radiates from within

I'm learning to be more honest with myself.

To base my worth not on my creations,
but on my ability to create.

To perceive my value not through other's validations,
but through my own affirmations.

To understand my beauty not as a societal standard,
but as self-love answered.

Have you lost yourself in pursuit of loving someone else?

Have you forgotten everything that you are?
Every skill that you possess?

Have you become so engulfed in the life of another that you've neglected everything that you love?

My friend, it's okay.

But I am here to remind you that who you are is not dependent on anyone else. Your worth, your purpose, and your future, is so fundamental; there is not a person in this world that can strip you of it.

Please, come back to yourself.

Your soul is aching for your affection.
Your body needs your nourishment.
Your heart is asking for attention.

Please, come back to yourself.

To feel truly loved by someone
for exactly who you are
is incredibly freeing and healing

However,
to attract such genuine love,
you must first choose
to love yourself.

Others will see your value
because you will know your value

We attract reflections
of who we think we are
and what we think we deserve

What makes a woman so beautiful, you ask?

I think it's the way she sparkles and shines,
the way she pours into others, the way she gives out her
time.

I think it's her smile, soft, steady, and sweet,
she gives it freely to all; she knows no defeat.

She wakes up every day, and thanks God for her life. She
pours water into plants; she knows wrong from right.

She loves people and all things, sour and sweet; she
gives grace to the bad and power to the weak.

She is brave and strong, humble, but proud;
she has the eyes of a fox, but the heart of a cloud.

She makes light out of darkness, and beauty out of
space. She marches to her own beat; she walks at her
own pace.

She's a woman who blooms in any dark room,
a woman who knows her worth. She creates art and
smiles, she runs for miles, she puts her light into the
earth.

She's a woman who looks her demons in the face,
a woman who needs no human embrace,
a woman resilient in every case,
a woman who walks through her life with grace.

So what makes a woman so beautiful, you ask?

I think it's the way that she shines.

I think it's the way she belongs only to herself,

the way she knows

she's absolutely

divine.

I'm grateful to have made a home in myself.

To have finally found the security I searched for
in the hands of others
for so long.

Every time the world becomes too big and too dark,
I retreat into my own arms,
knowing that there is indeed
a place in this world
that loves me

and *all my edges.*

To all my beautiful girls,

Take a deep breath in and a deep breath out.

As you read these words, think about what it is that you love most about yourself.

Reflect on your most cherished qualities.
Remind yourself of your intrinsic worth.

You deserve to feel loved by yourself. Your body deserves to be worshipped. Your heart deserves to be held. You are filled with infinite beauty, and you were divinely designed just as you are.

So please, loved one, be nice to yourself today.

Remind yourself of your perfect nature
and allow all your worries to drift away.

A poem to myself

Little girl with the pretty skin
Let me heal you from within
Let me remind you of your power
You are a heaven-picked flower

Little girl with the curly hair
Let me tell you my favorite prayer
I ask the Almighty to keep you safe
I know He'll comfort you in every way

Little girl with the broken heart
Your pain has blossomed into art
There is beauty that surrounds you
There is light that has found you

Little girl with the tearful eyes
You have won the grand prize
You are everything you always craved

You are the savior

and the saved

I think it's beautiful the way you try new things.

I think it's beautiful the way you persistently seek after yourself, opening your heart to every new experience. I think it's admirable that you've learned to love every part of yourself, especially the parts that you've spent years hiding from. I think it's brave the way you pour your heart into these words, the very heart that others have dismissed as too big or too bold. I think it's charming the way you offer love to this world, gently and honestly, yet always staying true to yourself.

I think it's fascinating the way you wake up every morning, unscathed by the fires of life, restlessly waiting for the next mountain to climb. I think it's lovely the way you perpetually find your way back to yourself, even after you've been lost in the hearts of others.

I think you are beautiful, every single side and bit. The way you love, the way you speak, the way you teach, the way you learn.

I think it's beautiful the way you try new things.

Season 8

Trust

What is it that you *really* want?

Do you want this life? Do you want this love?
Are you happy? Are you settling? Are you tired?

Ask yourself- *with honesty.*

Stop going through the motions.
Stop settling for what's in front of you.

Don't you see? This life is all you have. This moment,
this experience, the opportunities around you- it's here
and it's now and it's enticing and frightening and
frustrating all at the same time.

So please, stop doing the bare minimum. Stop wallowing
in your own discontentment. This life isn't going to slow
down for anyone. Your goals aren't going to manifest
overnight. Your relationships aren't going to blossom out
of mediocrity.

So, what is it then?
Is it you? Is it them?

What's your decision?
Are you going all in?

Or are you staying where you are?

Stop getting in your own way.

Oftentimes, when we grow up experiencing years of generational trauma, abuse, or adversity, we become subconsciously conditioned to our pain.

Whether that be a relationship that scarred you, a loved one that betrayed you, or a past that traumatized you- when we experience pain for a prolonged period of time, our brains become accustomed to our suffering, clinging onto our agony with every fiber.

And even when our life begins to blossom into a new and beautiful creation, we continue to subconsciously sabotage ourselves. We grasp onto our grief, we hide behind our hostility, we double-down on our downfall.

And in doing this, we create subliminal agreements with ourselves- that if we prepare for our future pain, we will soften the blow and expedite our anguish.

However, when you hold onto pain to protect yourself from disappointment, you only end up hurting yourself and prolonging your own problems.

You become the victim and the victimizer.
You become the abused and the abuser.

If you believe that you are not deserving of true peace,
not capable of true healing, or not equipped for true
blessings,

I am here to tell you:
You are worthy,
You are valuable,
And you are gifted.

Do not allow the pain of your past to determine the
direction of your destiny.

We are not shackled to our suffering.
We are not tied to our trauma.

Healing is possible. Growth is possible. And it is entirely
possible for you to live an abundant life, full of blessings
and prosperity.

But first, you must genuinely believe that you are
deserving and you are capable of transcending your
inequities.

Overthinking is one of our most destructive habits.

We overthink our pasts; we overthink our futures.
We overthink our careers, our decisions, our
relationships.

When we overthink, we create problems for ourselves
that are not real. We allow ourselves to wallow in what-
ifs and worst-case scenarios. And when we choose to
engage in this invisible grief, we choose to destroy our
current state of peace.

Instead, choose to take life day by day.

Allow experiences to flow through you. Give your
worries to God. Surrender to the future.

Rarely do things ever turn out as bad as we anticipated.

Are you hurting
or are you healing?

Are you grieving
or are you growing?

Are you overwhelmed with stress
or are you overcoming your struggles?

Perspective is everything.

Do not allow the circumstances of this season to drain
you, defeat you, or deplete you. Every situation we are
put into, every loss, every sorrow, every setback, is an
opportunity for us to grow. It is an opportunity for us to
reach into our depths and grasp onto ourselves with the
faith that we will *always* make it to the next step.

The more you begin to see your problems as
possibilities, the more power you will have over your
position.

So please, dear friend, shift your perspective, and watch
as your life becomes a beautiful reflection of everything
you desire.

Are you starving your soul, trying to feed your ego?

As you flow through life, you will encounter many formative moments, moments in which your true character and development will be put to test. These moments will come disguised as many faces and situations.

How do you behave when you feel triggered? Are you apologetic when you hurt someone you love? How do you react when a toxic flame from the past comes slithering back? How do you speak to yourself through seasons of failure and setback?

When moments as such arise, you will be faced with two fundamental decisions. One decision will fuel fire to your ego; it may make you feel powerful and superior at the moment.

On the contrary, the very opposite decision will feed your soul, it will nourish your heart and grow roots in your authenticity. And though the growing pains may initially cause you discomfort, it is only because your soul will be expanding.

This is precisely why, when we *only* make ego-based decisions, we do not achieve true spiritual growth.

An overpowering ego is the barrier between our bondage and our breakthrough.

However, when we make decisions that feed our soul, we become a vessel of growth, shedding light on our truest self. And as we continue to do this, our souls continue to level up.

So, ask yourself:

Are you starving your soul, trying to feed your ego?

Be patient with your journey

Some days as I sit here and write,
I tell you sweet things, and I remind you to fight

For what really matters, self-love and self-growth
I tell you to be strong; I tell you to have hope

The funny thing is,
As I spew my words and write my truths
I shed some tears, and I water my roots

I now peer in the past with a grateful heart
I can see through the fog
I no longer run from the dark

You see,
My words have been crafted by loss and despair
My poetry is filled with my loneliest prayers
My rhymes are rooted in my darkest nightmares
My verses born out of secrets I never shared

So, when I tell you to be strong
When I tell you to have hope
My words are not in vain

My words are the fruitful flowers

That have blossomed out of my pain

Everything starts small.

Our culture has fooled us into thinking that instant gratification is the way this world works. That big things come overnight, that dreams are achieved all at once.

But the truth is, good things take time, they take patience. They take the unshakeable faith that what you feel inside of yourself is so fundamentally true, there is not a person in this world that can strip you of it.

Keep going friend,

Time is *always* on your side.

It all begins with one.

One small step. One quick decision.
One big idea. One leap of faith.

It all begins with one.

Whether that be the beginning of a fruitful future, the
start of an exciting career, or the spark of a newfound
love- it all begins with one.

Think about it. All the decisions that we make- the big
ones, the little ones, the monotonous ones that get us
from day to day- those are the very decisions that have
the capacity to change us, to grow us, to transform our
world into something new.

The lady at your local coffee shop may be the
connection to your next blessing. The relationship you
always dreamed of may be waiting for you across the
globe.

The people that you meet,
The decisions that you make,
The desires that you have,

They are all intertwined in the fabric of your destiny.

Bet on yourself.
Visualize your success.
Believe in your potential.

Please know, you can accomplish anything that you authentically desire. God has deliberately deposited seeds in each and every one of our hearts. Whether that be a new idea, an innate gift, or a special interest, it is our responsibility to water those very seeds.

Focus on the now. Take small steps.
Set small goals. Cross those off your to-do list.
Be your biggest advocate. Do not become complacent.
Work on the next project. Move across the world.

No one else is going to live this life for you.

And I can promise you this, whether or not every goal you set becomes fruitful, you will never regret the inspiring journey of self-discovery.

You will be challenged. You will expand.
You will encounter incredible people along the way.

And most importantly, you will find God in every crevice of happiness and loneliness.

Continue to believe in yourself even when your current circumstances don't reflect what you *know* is possible.

The journey of your life is unfolding in continuous and intricate ways. Every season that you experience is necessary to shape you into the person you're called to be.

Your blessings are blossoming.
Your gifts are growing.
Your favor will soon become fruitful.

You may not tangibly see it yet, but I can assure you, something beautiful is cultivating below the surface.

Remember, God is the ultimate supplier.

He waters us with discomfort to help our roots grow deeper. He provides us with light to make our flowers bloom. He nourishes our souls with compassion and truth, so we can use our blessings in ways that will help others expand too.

Please understand, before you can receive all that He wants to give you, you must learn, you must awaken, you must grow outside of yourself. God is working behind the scenes, specially crafting each moment that will ultimately propel you into your dreams.

Trust in the process dear friend.

Your time is coming.

Season 9

Final Thoughts

Pursue your authentic self.

Do not compromise who you are, what you value, or the innate skills that you were given to mold into what society deems valuable.

If you perform only for the world,
you will lose yourself in the process.

Five Fundamental Truths

You're not always going to get the apology that you deserve.
Oftentimes, we must create closure for ourselves.

Life is temporary and so are people.
Free yourself from attachment to any outcome or relationship.

Peace of mind does not come from external circumstances or material goods.
You must create your own peace of mind through self-reflection, self-discovery, and divine connection.

Alone time is necessary.
Find pleasure in yourself.
You are the only permanent thing about your life.

Life is not fair.
Spend less time comparing and more time creating.

I think we ought to stop taking things so personally.

If someone can't love you the way you want to be loved- that has *nothing* to do with you. If someone doesn't treat you in the way that you desire to be treated- that is *not* a reflection of your worth.

We are all distinctive people- shaped and curved by life's experiences, treading through trying to find the answers. So, when you encounter people who can't love you, who can't see you, who can't understand you- please remember, that has nothing to do with who *you* are, but everything to do with who *they* are.

You will never be too much for the right person.

The person for you will learn to love you in all the ways you want to be loved. They will see you, understand you, and accept you.

But again, that will have nothing to do with *you*, but everything to do with finding the *right person.*

This is what I can promise you.

If you choose to avoid *true* self-reflection, the art of questioning your being, your intentions, your behaviors; you will a*lways* lose at life.

True victory comes from the ability to peer into ourselves with tender honesty. It comes in the moments of raw sincerity, when the veil is lifted and our ego shudders in the spotlight, when the content of our character becomes our most critical question.

And I can promise you this, it *will* make you uncomfortable. It will cause you to confront the regrets of your past and the intentions of your future. It may warrant a few apologies. It may call for some heavy conversations.

But that, my friend, means you have won. And you will *always* be winning. Because true victory does not come from the big house, the fancy car, or the successful career. To win at life is to have a heart that is pure and genuine. To have hands that pull others into safety. To have a voice that empowers, an essence that encourages, an aura that uplifts.

That is what I can promise you.

I am so in love

I am so in love with your mind,
the way it refreshes and restores

I'm in love your heart,
the way it gives, the way it pours

And I love your hands,
the way they comfort and console

And your energy,
always shining through your soul

I am so in love
with the person that you are,
the essence of your being

To deeply love yourself,

is absolutely freeing

Take care of yourself.

Wake up in the morning and thank God for your life.
Take a deep breath and set your intentions for the day.
Eat your breakfast and drink your coffee too. Get those 9
hours of sleep. Drink water. A lot of it. Be nice.
Compliment yourself. Focus on the things you love
about yourself. Work on the areas you'd like to see
change. Start that project. Make that phone call. Reach
out to your loved ones. Take a day off and see friends.
Tell someone you love them. Compliment a stranger.
Smile at a child. Read a good book. Have a good laugh.

Stretch.
Breathe.
Smile.
Pray.

Please, take care of yourself today.

What You Deserve

You deserve love in abundance.
You deserve an overflow of affection and inspiration.

You deserve joy.
You deserve to wake up every day with a clear mind and
a light heart.

You deserve success.
You deserve financial freedom, personal growth, and
spiritual connection.

You deserve companionship.
You deserve to be surrounded by meaningful and
uplifting relationships.

You deserve life.
You deserve the precious heartbeat that God has gifted
you.

Learn to enjoy the season that you're in.

The success will surely come.
The relationship will readily arrive.
The blessings will soon blossom.

And when they do, you will look back on your journey
and wish you had enjoyed the simplicity of your past.

Take a break. Have a snack.
Eat a cookie. Stretch your back.
Drink some water. Play a game.
Give a smile. Say your name.
Count your blessings. Pray to God.
Love a lot. Give a nod.
Call your mom. Text your friend.
Close your eyes. Play pretend.
Breathe your breaths. Love your skin.
Treat yourself. You'll always win.
Hug a girl. Kiss a boy.

There's a life here for you to enjoy.

I think we've all become addicts in some way.

Addicted to the thrills of life, addicted to the rat race, the flashy cars, the big opportunities, the breakthrough moments, the chaos of it all.

I think we've all become so concerned with living large that in the process, we've forgotten everything that makes us human. We've forgotten to love the little moments, the small nuggets of joy that keep us grounded to the earth. To sit in stillness and feel the warm pulse of our heartbeat, reminding us that we've been gifted another day. To drink tea next to someone we love and sit deeply in gratitude knowing that this very moment won't last forever. To watch the birds fly and the seasons change and the oceans rise and fall, understanding that we are such a small piece of this world, but nonetheless, we've continued to exist.

To live and to know.
To be still and to be slow.

When our life comes to a screeching halt, when time
stands still, when our world becomes dark with despair,
what is it that *really* matters to us?

In the moments of grieving loss, tragic accidents, fatal
diagnoses, what is it that we *truly* yearn for?

Is it our luxury leathers that keep us comforted in our
coldest moments? Do we find solace in our salaries, do
we find warmth in our wealth?

In those most desperate moments of humanity,
when life casts a shadow over our future,
what is it that we reach for?

The hands of another human.
The comfort of true connection.
The love from another's lips.

So, look around you. If you have even just one person
that brings this light into your life, you've already won,
my friend.

Don't let society tell you any different.

You have won.

I believe the phrase "ebb and flow" reflects the natural rhythm of life, the recurrent seasons of decline and regrowth that we all experience.

Everything in our life ebbs and flows: Money, love, relationships, stability, happiness, security, comfort. Life is a constant flow of these aspects coming and going, declining and regrowing. And I believe that the sooner we begin to accept this inevitable flow of life, the simpler our life becomes.

But, I think our natural inclination as humans is to resist these changes. So desperately, we want to cling onto what we know, what's comfortable, what feels easy and seamless. So, when a new season of life rolls in, we fight the changes, we refuse to accept the shifts that are trying to occur.

But what happens when we push back on motion?

Friction.

Instead of accepting the flow of life and trusting in the process, we worry, we get caught up in anxiety, we fight the very things that God is using to grow us. And as we do this, we wreak havoc on our own lives. We create friction within ourselves and within our relationships, and this friction bleeds into every piece of our world.